This Book l

CW00735646

THANK YOU

FOR PURCHASING THIS Easter Joke Book for Kids

PLEASE DON'T FORGET TO LEAVE US AN HONEST REVIEW AND SHARE WITH US YOUR EXPERIENCE AND HOW CAN HE IMPROVE EVEN MORE.

THANK YOU

FOR PURCHASING THIS Easter Joke Book for Kids

PLEASE DON'T FORGET TO LEAVE US AN HONEST REVIEW AND SHARE WITH US YOUR EXPERIENCE AND HOW CAN HE IMPROVE EVEN MORE.

Printed in Great Britain
by Amazon